Digital Writing for English Language Learners

Digital Writing for English Language Learners

Rusul Alrubail

ROWMAN & LITTLEFIELD
Lanham • Boulder • New York • London

Published by Rowman & Littlefield
A wholly owned subsidiary of
The Rowman & Littlefield Publishing Group, Inc.
4501 Forbes Boulevard, Suite 200, Lanham, Maryland 20706
www.rowman.com

Unit A, Whitacre Mews, 26-34 Stannary Street, London SE11 4AB

Copyright © 2017 by Rusul Alrubail

All rights reserved. No part of this book may be reproduced in any form or by any electronic or mechanical means, including information storage and retrieval systems, without written permission from the publisher, except by a reviewer who may quote passages in a review.

British Library Cataloguing in Publication Information Available

Library of Congress Cataloging-in-Publication Data Available

ISBN 978-1-4758-3109-2 (cloth : alk. paper)
ISBN 978-1-4758-3110-8 (pbk. : alk. paper)
ISBN 978-1-4758-3113-9 (electronic)

∞™ The paper used in this publication meets the minimum requirements of American National Standard for Information Sciences—Permanence of Paper for Printed Library Materials, ANSI/NISO Z39.48-1992.

Printed in the United States of America

I dedicate my first book to God almighty, to my two beautiful little girls, my loving husband, and supportive family.

Love and peace,
Rusul Alrubail

Contents

Foreword *Rosa Isiah, EdD*	ix
Introduction	1
1 Why Digital Writing for English Language Learners?	5
2 Digital Writing as Contextual Analysis	17
3 Where to Begin?	29
4 Digital Citizenship and Digital Writing	37
5 Creating a Culture of Connectivity	47
Final Thoughts	63
Bibliography	65
About the Author	69

Foreword

As a young English learner, writing was the most difficult subject for me and for many other language learners in my community. Ideas floated in my head, but I struggled to come up with the language and voice to communicate my thoughts effectively. Writing can be a challenge for students and especially for English learner students who are trying to accommodate their ideas, feelings, and position in a new schooling system. New-to-the-country English learners, as well as long-term English learners, continue to have similar struggles with writing. As educators, we have the responsibility to create and provide our students with tools and mediums that support self-expression, including writing.

There are limited resources available to those of us who seek to provide engaging and innovative differentiated instruction for English learners. Rusul Alrubail is one of those resources. She teaches, speaks, and writes about supports for our English learner community. Rusul is someone I seek when I need ideas and resources that will support my students and my personal learning. As a connected educator who is passionate about student agency, culture, and language, Rusul is a game changer and dedicated advocate for our EL students. I'm not surprised that she has taken this writing opportunity to highlight the benefits of digital literacy in education as a writing resource and tool for educators and students. If this is your introduction to Rusul's work, then congratulations! You won't be disappointed.

This book provides insight into Rusul's understanding of the needs of English learners. She addresses everything you may wonder about, including getting started, platforms to use, and the alignment of the Common Core standards. Rusul also includes information on student privacy, student voice, and educator cultural competency.

Writing is a place where students can express and establish voice, agency, and creativity. I'm thankful that Rusul is providing the teaching and learning community with a valuable instructional writing resource. I'm sure you'll enjoy and appreciate her work as much as I do.

Rosa Isiah, EdD
Principal, Presenter, and Agent of Change

Introduction
On Digital Writing

Writing has become a fluid concept in education. It not only encompasses traditional forms of writing—articles, essays, reports—but it also can imply the act of reflection, responses, debates, question and answer, and blogging. Blogging; microblogging; tweeting; and using Instagram, Snapchat, and any other social media platforms have become a twenty-first-century digital tool to be used to connect, collaborate, share, and learn from people all around the world.

Educators from across the globe blog to share their teaching and learning in the classroom. Blogging is a way to document, reflect, and share pedagogical strategies and teaching tools used in the classroom. With the benefits of blogging as a reflective teaching tool, why not use this tool with our students in the classroom?

Teachers are integrating blogging as a communicative storytelling mode for students to share stories, thoughts, ideas, responses, discussions, and many other types of communication in the classroom.

WHAT IS BLOGGING?

Blogging is a digital communication mode that often incorporates elements of digital and social media to deliver a reflective response about a subject, person, event, or circumstance. Blogging provides an opportunity for students to engage meaningfully with different modes of digital literacies. Blogging involves creating a website and publishing posts on it. Blogs are very loose in definition, and there's a lot of room to be creative and establish what blogging may mean to you and your students.

Blogs can be anywhere from text, articles, short reflection pieces, and essays to plans, goals, strategies or tips, how-tos, images, and poetry. Blogging is limitless in terms of structure. As a result, a blog can be an image or video with a thought-provoking caption. It can be a beautiful quote with thoughts strung to it. It can also be a digital story that moves the reader to think, reflect, and feel.

A study conducted by Advanced Placement and The National Writing Project found that three-quarters of teachers believe the use of Internet and digital tools has an "overall positive impact" on students' research habits and communication skills (Purcell et al. 2012). Another study on the impact of digital tools on students' writing also found that "96% agree that digital technologies 'allow students to share their work with a wider and more varied audience'" (Purcell, Buchanan, and Friedrich 2013).

Clearly, exposing students to different modes of technologies can play a huge factor in developing and shaping their thoughts and ideas. By providing the opportunity for students to communicate in a framework of multiliteracies, we can even begin to see improvement in their research, writing, and critical thinking skills (Purcell, Buchanan, and Friedrich 2013). Blogging needs to be seen as a "formal" mode of writing because it provides an opportunity for students to engage in reading and writing and in turn to strengthen communication skills. Digital writing for English language learners (ELL) can provide students the platform, space, and opportunity for social, cultural, and communicative support.

I chose to concentrate on digital writing for English language learners because, often in an ELL classroom, teachers need to modify certain writing activities and assignments to meet the learners' needs. Blogging, among other activities, can be a very flexible method to use when modifying writing and communication assignments. Due to the fact that blogging itself is very subjective, the assignments can often be tailored and be representative of the student's thoughts and ideas while still enhancing students' writing skills.

LEARNING OBJECTIVES

By the end of this book you will understand:

- the benefits of digital writing,
- how digital writing can help English language learners,
- how to start writing digitally with your students,
- rights and privacy concerns, and
- how to create a culture and community of connectivity through blogging or digital portfolios.

CHAPTER 1

Why Digital Writing for English Language Learners?

DIGITAL COMMUNICATION: WHAT THE RESEARCH SAYS

Did you know that the Internet's use between 2005 and 2013 increased by 85 percent? This means that 72 percent of online adults and 80 percent of online teens use social network sites (Zickuhr 2013, 1–26). However, with these staggering statistics, it still does not mean that everyone has digital access. A recent study suggests that only 37 percent of teens own a smartphone, while about 78 percent of them own a cell phone. This is an indicator that online access comes in different forms. It also indicates that, in the classroom, we should be mindful of who has access to the Internet and who does not. Digital equity is an issue that affects many schools and districts, and as educators, when choosing and creating lesson plans, we should keep in mind our expectations of students and the digital access they have to complete assignments.

The Pew Research Center's Internet and American Life Project, in collaboration with the College Board and the National Writing Project, conducted a survey to see the impact of digital tools on students' writing and how writing is taught in schools. Half of the teachers (50 percent) say that digital tools make it easier for students to write (National Writing Project and Pew Research Center 2013). This number proves that digital tools have become almost necessary to use in the classroom to further students' writing and communication. Moreover, 40 percent of the surveyed teachers said that their students already share their work publicly using wikis, blogs, and websites. Consequently, blogging has become a powerful tool for students to communicate their thoughts and ideas digitally.

With that being said, teachers still see the downside of using digital tools in the classroom. One of the worries that educators have regarding using digital tools in the classroom is that it will affect the quality of students' work; "68% of these teachers say digital tools make students more likely—as opposed to less likely or having no impact—to take shortcuts and not put effort into their writing" (National Writing Project and Pew Research Center 2013). Some other hesitations for using digital tools in the class suggested that 46 percent of teachers say digital tools make students more likely to "write fast and be careless" (National Writing Project and Pew Research Center 2013).

The idea that digital writing increases grammatical and structural errors is not without reason. Many social media and digital tools encourage abbreviated writing; however, those platforms, with the right pedagogical use, can also encourage brevity, clarity, and creativity in writing. For example, Instagram is a photo-sharing platform that is very popular among youth and can be used as a storytelling tool in the classroom. Teachers can encourage students to share photos that they feel connected to and are passionate about and write short essays about them. Using Instagram in this way encourages students to be creative and detailed in their writing. More importantly, by using Instagram as a microblogging platform, students get to share their passions with their teachers and their peers, and teachers can engage students to write and share their work with others.

Teachers can still provide feedback on structure and grammar, but the focus now is the content, which is equally important. When teachers work closely with students to provide feedback on their writing, students can see that it is equally important to care about their digital writing as much as they care about their analog writing. In fact, feedback encourages them to care more about their communication skills as a whole because they are writing for a wider audience.

Digital writing—including blogging, microblogging, writing on social media platforms, and tweeting—also allows students to gain

Table 1.1.

These AP and NWP teachers tend to rate students' specific writing skills as "good" or "fair"

Overall, how would you rate your students in their ability to do each of the following?

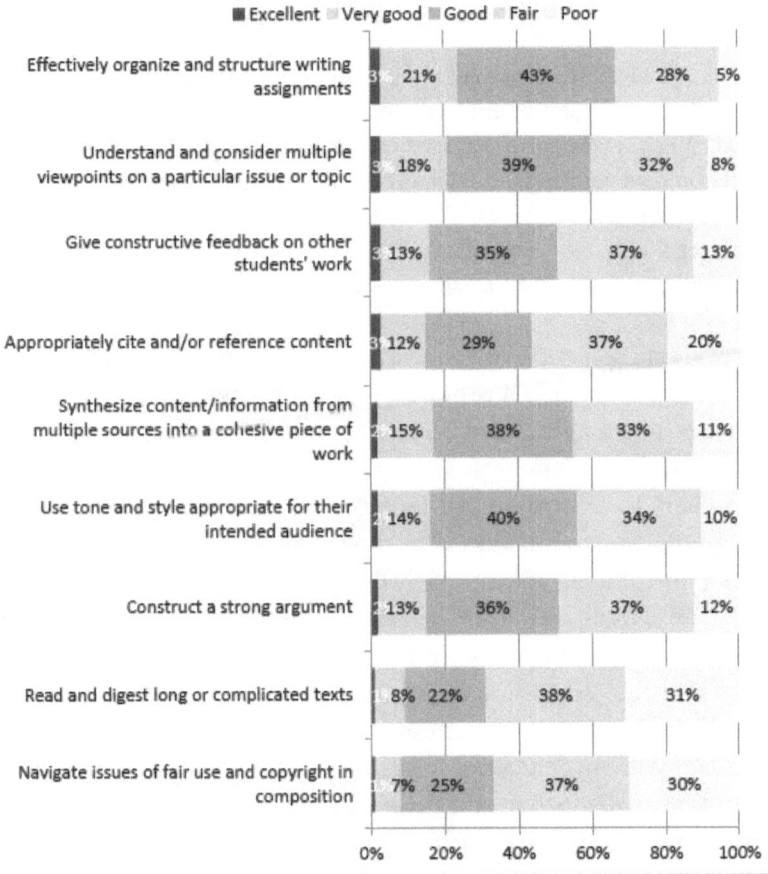

Source: The Pew Research Center's Internet & American Life Project Online Survey of Teachers, March 7 to April 23, 2012. Based on a non-representative sample of 2,067 middle and high school teachers.

access and control of their own learning. Students who communicate their learning online can see the wide opportunities that are available to them, and in turn, they start to value those opportunities. Research suggests that allowing students to write digitally empowers them by providing them a choice.

> Use of social software such as blogs and wikis can empower learners and provide greater learner control through learner-learner interaction. When learners use the shared online space to build their learning environment collaboratively in a wiki, the choice made by the teacher to delegate control to the students in turn increases the students' choices within that context, and their ability to manage structure and dialogue. (Benson and Samaraswickrema 2007)

By providing students with choices, teachers encourage engagement and interactivity when it comes to writing. Students, as a result, will feel very passionate about learning, writing, and communicating altogether.

Teachers have a reason to be worried about introducing digital tools in the classroom. However, those worries and hesitations cannot stop us from introducing tools that our students are already using daily. These tools aren't just tools to be used for the sake of it; technology is such an impactful, relevant, and necessary component in the twenty-first-century learning environment. And while integrating it in the classroom can shift pedagogy, we must be able to move and adapt with this change.

There are pedagogical strategies that can ensure teachers help students to use digital writing tools to their utmost potential; these strategies are discussed further in this book. Moreover, like anything, when we use something we aren't accustomed to, we can easily not use its full potential. Implementing digital tools in the classroom needs to be intentional, which means that educators need effective lesson plans specifically based on their learning outcomes and that introduce the tools as a means to meet those learning outcomes. In this way, the use of digital tools is specific, precise, and clear for both teachers and students. Planning lessons around learning outcomes and combining those outcomes with the appropriate tool is really important to ensure that learning outcomes are met and that the tools are being used for a specific reason.

There is also a compelling amount of research that argues the importance of using digital tools for students not only to improve communication skills but also to invest in social and cultural interaction. Social and cultural interactions are necessary elements to implement in English language classrooms. McLoughlin and Lee (2007) argue that social and cultural interactions are pedagogical tools that can be leveraged in the classroom. In fact, they are "pedagogical tools that stem from their *affordances* of sharing, communication and information discovery."

As a result, social and cultural interactions are pedagogical tools themselves to help English language learners to connect, learn, and share their thoughts and ideas about their experiences. In later chapters of this book, there are some strategies to implement social and cultural themes in the classroom along with digital writing to ensure that English language learners have an opportunity to explore different cultures and share ideas about their own cultures in a safe and nurturing environment.

BLOGGING AS COMMUNICATIVE PRACTICE

Communicative practice is an approach to teaching and learning a language that centers on interaction as one of the main goals of learning. Why is interaction so important in language learning? When students learn a new language, it's important for them to apply it right away in social settings in order to better grasp the context of the language. Learning the language through interaction is also a motivating and engaging way to learn for students. They are more inclined to remember vocabulary, grammar, and structure when they know how to use it in real-world conversations and interactions.

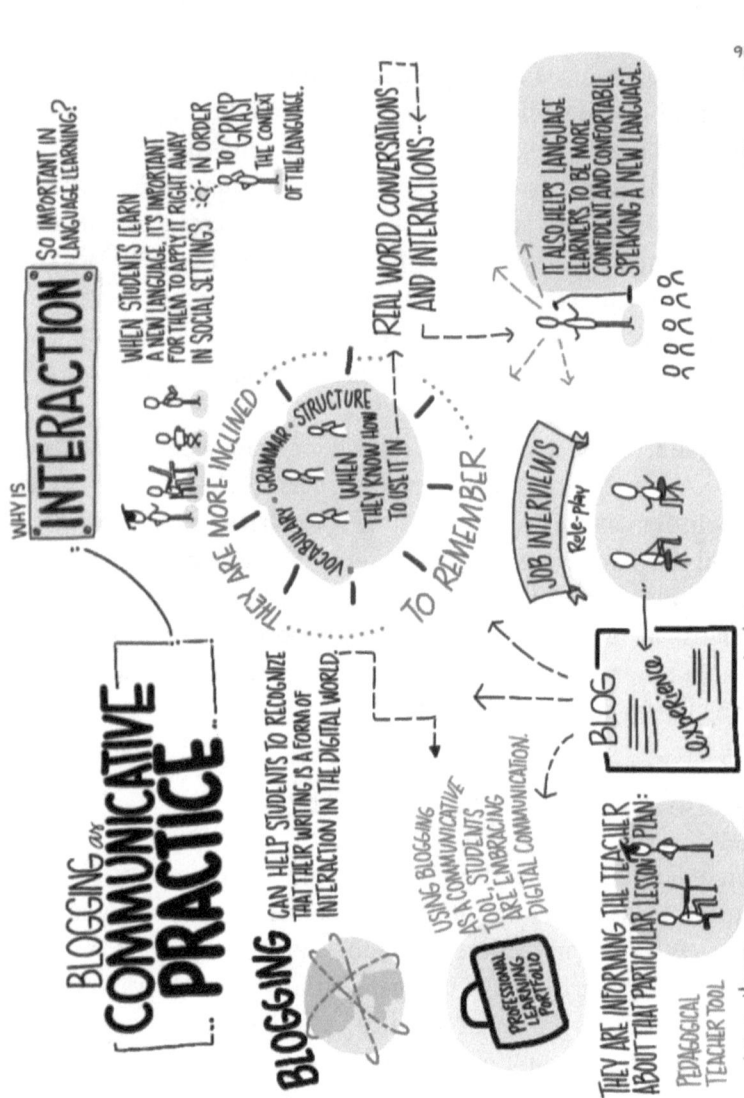

Figure 1.1. Blogging as Communicative Practice.
Image by Rebeca Zuñiga, September 2016.

Another reason interaction is so vital when learning a language is because it helps language learners to be more confident and comfortable speaking the new language. More practice ensures that students can overcome the initial hesitation and discomfort when speaking the new language. The more they have conversations and write as a form of communicative practice, the more they see the language as a tool to help them to achieve their communication goals. For example, English language learners can learn more about job interviews by roleplaying with their peers in an interviewer-interviewee conversation.

But let's take that to the next level of communicative practice. Students can then blog about their interview experience. In this way, students can reflect on their own communicative practice and provide insight on how they can improve next time. What is really important in this practice is that, by having students blog about their experiences, they are informing the teacher about that particular lesson plan: what worked for them, what could have been done differently. In a way, student blogging can be used as a tool for pedagogical teacher reflection, where teachers can read about students' experiences with lessons and how they can adjust and improve according to the students' learning needs next time.

Blogging helps students to see that the language is a tool to communicate with other people in social settings. It can also help them to recognize that their writing is a form of interaction in the digital world. This realization will help them in the long run when building their professional learning portfolio online. By using blogging as a communicative tool, students are embracing digital communication, which in turn opens different pathways and opportunities for them.

When starting blogging with students, it's important to provide them with various opportunities to write, share, and reflect on their own classroom experiences. To help students to communicate their thoughts and ideas effectively when blogging, provide them with the following tips:

1. *Be yourself.* When blogging, make sure that students remember to be themselves and do not to try to use anyone else's

voice. Many students will ask you to provide a writing sample or an example of a blog post about the topics you assign. Sometimes these examples actually hinder students' writing instead of motivating them to write. They can get so caught up in emulating the example that they forget their own voice is just as good or even better.

2. *Be clear and concise.* Blogs are made for quick reads. Most often, blogs more than seven hundred words are not read in full. Remind students to keep blogs short and simple. This should help English language learners to focus on writing their points and should also help them to use vocabulary words with which they're comfortable. Writing in point form also helps many English language learners to get over the hurdle of language block, where they know what they like to write but get overwhelmed that they don't have enough to say.

3. *Don't worry about grammar and structure.* The beauty of blogging is that most often readers are familiar with the idea that blogs are written in a quick manner. Many readers skip over any typos and spelling errors in blogs. That does not mean that students should not edit their work. They should, in fact, go over their blog posts a few times before publishing. However, students should not stress over grammar and sentence structure to a point where they're not comfortable publishing their work. Remind students that communicating their point should be the ultimate goal, and with practice, their grammar and sentence structure will improve naturally.

4. *Write about topics you like.* This is only possible if teachers are willing to give the reins to students when choosing topics to write about. Many students feel uninspired by topics that we choose for them. It's important that students have the opportunity to write about topics they like and are interested in. In many cultures, students are taught to go by the teacher's lead on the topics, so it's important to provide extra encouragement for English language learners to find and search for a topic they

like. This might be a process of brainstorming with the students some possibilities or talking about their interest with other students to discover and explore some future writing topics.
5. *Use first-person pronouns.* How often do we tell students not to use *I* or *me* in writing? We tend to steer them clear of first-person pronouns in writing for many reasons: It takes away from the strength of their arguments, it makes a statement subject, it does not sound professional, and many other reasons. However, when it comes to blogging and English language learners, encourage them to use the *I* pronoun. This will help them with the flow of their ideas. For example, many students feel comfortable starting a sentence with "I think" or "I believe" or "In my opinion." It is perfectly fine for them to do that because blogging is a self-reflective mode of writing.

Communicative practices have a real-life purpose, and as a result, when assigning blogs, make sure that they have a purpose and a connection to communication practices that we do in the real world. Some of these practices may include:

- obtaining information about a person, place, or event;
- discussing culture, events, or issues; and
- sharing information about oneself or others.

There are many benefits to using communicative-style learning in the classroom, and the benefits far outweigh the challenges.

Examples of communicative activities that teachers can assign for blogging include the following:

- *Letters:* These can be a letter-to-the-editor assignment or a letter from a concerned citizen. In letter assignments, students are asked to choose a public issue, story, or event that they care about; reflect on reactions, news articles, and so on; and write their own letters to their chosen individuals.

Table 1.2.

Benefits of Using Communicative Pedagogy in the Classroom	The Challenges of Using Communicative Pedagogy in the Classroom
• More exposure to Target Language. • More authentic opportunities to *use* the language. • Engaging and inspiring for learners. • Provides opportunity to use authentic materials. • Exposure to various cultural communications: clichés, slang, accent, etc. • Students seeing the relevancy of learning the target language.	• Teachers need to know how to offer support and meet the individual learning needs of students. This can mean more time is needed for planning and preparation of activities. • Communicative activities can pose challenges in assessment. • There might be some pushback from learners who are accustomed to teacher-centred pedagogy.

This chart is adapted from *Best of Bilash: Improving Second Language Education*, 2011.

- *How-to Guides:* Many blogs cover a lot of how-to topics. Blogs by nature are short, concise, and interactive. How-to guides are very easy for readers to understand and are relevant and applicable. Have students write a how-to guide about something they enjoy doing. Have them come up with catchy titles: "How to Catch More Pokemons: A Step-by-Step Guide on How to Play *Pokemon Go*" or "How to Be an Entrepreneur Using Instagram."
- *Movie/TV Show Reviews:* Instead of having students summarize articles or essays, have them review movies, TV shows, or books that they've watched and read recently. Ask them the following questions: What was this movie, show, or book about? What did you think of this piece of work? What was one part you enjoyed about it, and what was one part you didn't enjoy? Would you recommend this movie, show, or book to your friends and family? Blogging about what they're reading and watching not only allows for students to share their interest through writing but also allows teachers and students to connect with each other using social and cultural conversations.

SAMPLE BLOGGING ASSIGNMENT

In this assignment, you are required to create a blog that represents you and your own opinions. This blog will be used to write blog posts related to class discussions about the topics and articles we have read and discussed. We will be using *The Writing Project*.

Feel free to have fun with personalizing the blog, and make it really representative of who you are as a person and as a student in the digital world. Remember to keep it professional and to refrain from using offensive language. Your blogging platform can be used after the completion of the course to help you with branding yourself and to stay relevant in the digital space. Think of it as a great start to a professional writing portfolio.

Instructions

You will write seven to eight blog entries throughout the semester, but you will be graded on only five of your choice. You will be graded on:

- the overall appearance of the blog, including the interface and if there are any additional related images or videos,
- professionalism, and
- five of your best posts (chosen posts need to be at least three hundred words).

Content of the Posts

Content should be driven through a self-reflection on your own learning:

- Does the post incorporate issues discussed in class?
- Does the post pose a few questions about the issue being discussed?
- How do you relate information and knowledge gained from classroom discussions to the self-reflection process?

CHAPTER 2

Digital Writing as Contextual Analysis

BLOGGING FOR SOCIAL AND CULTURAL SUPPORT

All students need social and cultural support in the classroom. For English language learners, this need is amplified due to the language barrier, social and cultural changes and shifts, and many other factors. So while implementing culturally responsive teaching is important in classrooms, it is *especially* needed in a classroom with English language learners. Social and cultural support for English language learners can come in many forms, and digital writing can help with this. Blogging, specifically, opens pathways for students to learn about one another's social and cultural norms, and more importantly, students end up connecting with one another.

The big question remains: How do we leverage blogging as a tool to connect the teacher and students socially and culturally? As previously stated, blogging helps students to develop an understanding and appreciation of each other's social and cultural practices. It also helps to break down barriers between different cultural beliefs, and even more so, it helps to shatter stereotypes that we often have about different societies and cultures.

For example, one of my students chose to focus the subject of his digital story on his country. He created the story to tell his classmates and everyone watching a little bit about how life was back home. Consequently, by providing an opportunity for students to write and create digital work about their cultures, a teacher is opening pathways to global learning and connections with her students. There are several ways to help students blog about social and cultural issues that are relevant to their situations and everyday lives.

Blogging about Informational Text

Provide a piece of informational text to the class, and ask students to reflect on how the piece relates or does not relate to their beliefs, values, and cultures. Ask the students to reflect on the following questions:

- What is the main point of the text?
- In your own words, describe the point of view of the author.
- Do you agree or disagree with the author's point of view? Why or why not?
- How are the points mentioned in the article similar to your own ideas or beliefs about the topic? How are the points different?

Encourage students to relate the topic to their own experiences, backgrounds, and cultures:

- Have you, or do you know anyone who . . . ?
- Personally, what do you think of . . . ?

Blogging about Short Stories

Short stories are often complex pieces for English language learners, so it's important for them to have a platform where they can share their thoughts and ideas about the stories they read. Stories often carry social and cultural messages. By encouraging students to see how they connect to the stories' messages, they will not only be active readers, but they will also start to critically think about the issues in the stories and how they connect to them. Consider guiding them with the following questions:

- Who is the main character in the story? Why do you think he or she is the main character?
- What are some of the themes highlighted in the story?
- What are the themes you connected with most? Why?

- What are some of the themes you connected with least? Please explain your answer.
- Describe some of the story's similarities to your own culture.
- Describe some of the story's differences from your own culture.

Some questions based on content can start with:

- Why do you think the character did . . . ?
- How would you have reacted or behaved in this situation . . . ?
- Can you share a story or an experience where you felt like . . . ?

When you're creating the questions to guide students through the reading, it's best to start with *who, what, when, where,* and *how.* These questions will help students to summarize and describe the text. Next, to push the students to critically think and analyze the text, ask the students these two questions: Why is this important? Why do we need to know this piece of information? These questions will help students to form their own opinions about the topic or issue and to engage critically with the text. Students can reflect on these discussion questions with their classmates before they begin writing. In this way, when they write, they can also incorporate some of the class discussion and the points that were made by their peers.

Before they begin to blog, make sure to remind students that they do not have to answer the questions you provided in order. In fact, they don't even have to answer the questions! If they feel passionate about the topic, then they can discuss it without using the discussion prompts. Many English language learners will prefer to use the questions you pose, and that's fine. With encouragement and practice, they can begin to reflect on the topic without having to use question prompts.

Remember that the questions need to relate back to the students and their own experiences with the topic or issue that is being discussed. To help students to write ideas that flow together, encourage them to take the questions that they answered out of the blog. They can use them as a guide while writing, but once they complete the blog post, have them delete the questions before they publish it. In this way, their blog looks like a reflective piece of writing instead of just a question-and-answer post.

Show the students the significance of putting their ideas together in one paragraph by having them read their paragraphs before they publish them. They can read aloud to another peer or read to themselves. By encouraging students to look at their answers as a whole paragraph, you're also encouraging them to write long forms of writing and responses, which will prepare them for research and literary essays later on.

BLOGGING AND VISUAL LITERACY

Whether staring at a blank page or a new post, starting to write can be a very overwhelming task for most writers. English language learners experience this difficulty often. Using visuals as writing prompts can ease students into writing and blogging. Using visuals as modes of writing, a prompt for writing, or an extension to writing can motivate and engage students in the process of writing. Visuals can also help students to practice close reading and critical thinking. The following are ways to incorporate visuals with blogging.

Visuals as Storytelling Prompts

Provide images and pictures of interesting things, or even better, have the students pick out their own images and pictures. Ask students to write a narrative about the image. Some questions they might consider are:

- Who or what is in the picture? Write a story that gives the background about this picture.
- What is the subject doing?
- What's so special about the subject?

- What was or is currently happening in the image?
- What will happen after?

About-Me Visuals

Have students choose an image or a photograph that means something to them. Ask students to write a blog post sharing the meaning of the chosen image:

- What does this image mean to you?
- Why is it so important?
- What does that say about you?
- How does this image help us to understand who you are as a person?
- If you could go back and change anything about the image's situation, circumstance, or relation to you, would you? Why or why not?

Instagram Storytelling

This is a little similar to the previous assignment, but it also combines the use of social media and blogging. Ask students to choose a picture of theirs or anyone else's, and have them tell a story about that picture.

- Describe the picture.
- Where is the setting?
- Who are the main subjects or characters in the picture?
- What does the picture tell us about the subjects?
- Why did you choose this picture?
- What is it about this picture that spoke to you?
- What is the purpose of this picture? How can you tell?

Remember that students can choose any picture from any social media platforms they're connected with, of course while making sure that the pictures are not offensive and do not break any of the school's social media policies.

Visual Description

This activity may be suitable for younger students. Ask students to describe their chosen photo:

- What are the colors, scheme, layout, shapes, and so on?

This activity helps with vocabulary knowledge and comprehension as well as description.

By providing opportunities for students to incorporate visual literacy in blogging, students will begin to see the benefits of writing and communicating their thoughts and ideas. They will see that their writing is applicable in the real world and will be engaged and motivated to write.

Close-Reading Visuals

Practicing close-reading is another benefit to using visuals in writing. Students are pushed to think critically about all the visual elements and how they're combined to create one whole picture. Students will be close-reading the visuals to identify the main components of an image.

Using visual texts as a form of literacy helps to support English language learners with their newfound vocabulary and sentence structure. It also helps them to practice communicative writing. Using visuals as literacy also allows the teacher to personalize learning for the students to meet their learning needs. Many students will find that looking at and assessing visuals before writing helps to get the ideas and stories to flow, which is one way to avoid writer's block.

PEDAGOGICAL AND PEER FEEDBACK

We learned in chapter 1 about the benefits of blogging for the teacher, and it often comes in a variety of forms. One of the most important benefits that teachers notice after students start blogging is pedagogical feedback. When students blog about their learning, they also inherently discuss their takes on the lesson and what went on in the classroom that day. This helps the teacher to see and identify areas to help students meet their individual learning needs.

More importantly, this feedback is vital to improve the teacher's pedagogy. By seeing how students benefited or didn't benefit from the lesson, the teacher can implement changes in her teaching style and methodology in the next lesson, ensuring that each student's learning needs are being met with personalized pedagogy.

Blogging can bridge the communication gap between the teacher and students. Many students, especially English language learners, have a hard time sharing their learning progress or lesson reflection with the teacher.

Blogging can also merge face-to-face communication with digital communication. If a student is not comfortable having a face-to-face conversation because of a lack of confidence in his or her oral skills, shyness, or cultural barriers, then the teacher can encourage him or her to write a blog post to reflect on how the lesson went.

Here are some questions to help students provide lesson feedback through digital writing:

1. What did you learn in the classroom today?
2. Did you enjoy the lesson? Why or why not?
3. What are some things you'd like to change about this topic or subject?
4. What would you like to learn about next time?
5. What is a topic that you're interested in but that we haven't yet learned about in class?

It's important to frame the questions to better understand the student's process of learning—what they're learning and, more importantly, how they're learning. Our classrooms will only improve if we seek feedback to be better. When teachers frame the questions to make them about the students' learning, they are able to learn more about students and to understand and empathize with their perspectives, concerns, and needs.

As a result of providing teacher feedback, students will start to experience *metacognitive learning*, a process of being actively aware of one's own learning and taking active control of one's learning strategies (Son, Kenna, and Pfirman 2007). In order to experience metacognitive learning, it's not enough to be aware of one's own learning; it's also important to identify the strategies that work well for oneself (Son, Kenna, and Pfirman 2007). Therefore, there needs to be a process to identify learning goals and a plan to meet those goals.

Relating to the pedagogical feedback, students need to be encouraged to identify what they're learning and which strategies are working for them when it comes to learning concepts. When they identify the strategies that work for them, inevitably they will provide the teacher with feedback on the pedagogical approach needed to meet their learning goals. For example, a student can provide the following: "I really liked how we used those videos last time to look at the way speakers deliver their main idea to the audience." This feedback tells the teacher that this student found the video and audio useful, and maybe next time, it might also help them to grasp other concepts.

PEER FEEDBACK

The National Commission on Writing and Pew Research Center conducted a survey about writing, technology, and teens. What they found was that teens write an overwhelming amount. They do so, though, on social media and with their peers, and they very much enjoy doing it (Lenhart et al. 2008). If students are willing to write more on social media and with their peers, then why not incorporate that in the classroom? Digital writing provides a great opportunity for students to connect with their peers and to consult each other on their own writing. There are several ways to incorporate peer feedback into your classroom. The following are some tips and suggestions to share with students when starting the peer feedback process.

Set the Tone

Make sure students understand why they're reading and editing each other's work. This could be explained at the beginning of the lesson. Help students to see that the process is really so that they all benefit from each other's writing styles, ideas, and stories.

Lay Some Ground Rules

Of course students should be trusted to make the best judgments; however, it's also important to remind students that editing and providing feedback to their peers is not about judging their peers. Help them to see the difference between judgmental criticism and judgmental feedback. Here is an example:

- *Poor feedback:* "You have lots of grammar errors."
- *Good feedback:* "Make sure to revise your comma use in the first paragraph."

Feedback Needs to Be Specific

Remind students that vague feedback with no examples can hinder their peers' writing instead of improve it. Feedback needs to be specific, with an example in order for it to be truly constructive:

- *Poor feedback:* "Your main idea is vague."
- *Good feedback:* "Your thesis statement can be stronger if you explain why this should matter to the reader."

Positive-Constructive-Positive (PCP)

Remind students to structure their comments in a PCP sandwich, which means that the first comment should be positive to highlight something great that stood out to them throughout the piece of writing. The second comment should offer constructive feedback: What can the author do to make their piece better? The constructive feedback should follow the previous tips regarding tone, specificity, and so on. Then the last comment should highlight something else that is strong in the piece that stood out to the reader. The last comment could be a general comment regarding the whole piece, or it could be a specific one about a practice that they should continue to do in their writing.

For example: "Your thesis statement did a wonderful job of explaining elements that will be used to support your argument. Try to find more supportive evidence to include in your paragraphs to support your main idea. Your conclusion was very creative and offered a different perspective!"

Feedback Categories

Provide the students with categories for feedback. For example, there can be three categories for students to assess, such as grammar and sentence structure, creativity, and evidence. Of course, make sure that the categories they're reviewing were first introduced to students when they wrote the assignment. That way the requirements and outcomes are aligned when doing the peer feedback.

Anabel Gonzalez (2016), a secondary ESL teacher in North Carolina, suggests using inquiry-based learning for students to understand their peers' work. This means that, instead of automatically correcting and giving feedback, students can ask questions about their peers' work. This encourages students to think critically about each other's writing and writing that they generally read. It also encourages students to take a step back and not jump to their own conclusions about their peers' writing.

Here are several prompts for question-driven peer feedback:

- Why did you write about this topic, issue, or event?
- What did you mean by this statement _____?
- When you say this, do you mean _____? Rephrase here _____.
- Why did you choose this as an example to support your idea?
- How do you feel about this paragraph relating to the whole piece?
- How do you feel overall about your piece? Which areas do you feel confident about? Which areas need more work?

CHAPTER 3

Where to Begin?

CLASSROOM BLOGS VERSUS STUDENT BLOGS

The decision to develop a classroom blog or individual student blogs really depends on the teacher and their purpose for using blogging. Like most digital tools, each type of blog has a specific purpose and meets specific learning outcomes. Therefore, before implementing blogging with your students, it's important to think about the goal you wish to accomplish with blogging. Here are some questions to determine what the purpose of blogging may be in your classroom and which blogging platform is more suitable for you and your students:

- Why do you want to blog with your students?
- What do you hope your students will learn throughout their blogging journeys?
- Will your students blog a few times a week, or will they blog less than that?
- Will you prefer if one student updates the classroom blog every day or week?
- Is tracking the students' writing progress an important thing for you?

The following are a few platform suggestions for classroom blogs and student blogs.

Blogger

Blogger is Google's blogging platform. The interface is very easy to use. It's customizable with different themes, colors, and templates.

Table 3.1. Content Suggestions for Classroom Blogs & Student Blogs

Classroom Blogs	Student Blogs
• Featured student of the week/day • Classroom calendar with due dates, birthdays, culture holidays, and events. • Important notices/messages. • Classroom rules/guidelines for blogging. • Pictures of classroom activities/projects (with parent permission to publish) • Interesting articles, stories, current event posts. • Social media stream/widget (Twitter, Instagram, Facebook). • Subscribe button/link.	• Student reflections (daily/weekly) on lessons, learning and school experience. • Opinion pieces on current events. • Letter to the editor. • Sharing a passion project. • Fiction writing. • Book reviews. • Movie/TV show reviews. • Digital Storytelling. • Video Log. • Literary analysis of plays, novels, poetry they read in class. • Image analysis. • Free writing.

What Should We Write on Classroom & Student Blogs?

It also has a public and private feature, where you can keep your blog private if you choose. It's free to use for everyone.

Wordpress

Wordpress is a little more detailed and contains more options in terms of customization, themes, and layout. Students could use Wordpress for their student blogs, but it might be best for older students (grade 11 through college). It also offers a yearly subscription plan if you choose the ad-free interface.

EduBlogs

EduBlogs contains options for educators to use the blog for their classrooms, schools, colleges, and universities. The basic free version offers a few options, but if a teacher is looking to have students manage the blogs—including many features like embedded videos, plugins, and so on—then there is a monthly or a yearly subscription plan available.

Write About

Write About is a platform for teachers and students to write on. The platform is free to use but also contains a yearly subscription option for such added features as student–teacher sharing, analytics, and more. Another feature on Write About, under the "Ideas" section on their site, is lots of inspiring prompts, stories, and lessons to use with students when blogging.

The Writing Project

The Writing Project is a platform for student voice and teacher communities. It provides a safe classroom community to be made either private or public. The platform contains several writing options: The first is free narrative writing for students; the second is essay writing; and the third is paragraph writing. Both the essay- and paragraph-writing options provide a smart tool to guide students through inquiry prompts to compose strong argumentative and literary writing. The Writing Project is also a community of student and teacher voices to empower advocacy in education about culturally relevant topics.

SOCIAL MEDIA TOOLS

Instagram

Instagram is a photo-sharing and video-sharing platform. Accounts can be made public or private. When you share a photo on Instagram, you have an option of adding a description along with the photo. This is a great opportunity for teachers to practice storytelling with Instagram.

Task:

1. Ask students to choose a photo that means something to them.
2. Ask them to write two to three sentences describing the objects of the photo. Who or what is in the photo? What are they doing? Where is the setting?

3. Next, have students explain in two to three sentences what the photo means to them. Why is the photo important? What is significant about the photo? What connects them to it?
4. Categorizing and tagging are also important features of Instagram. Have students tag their photos with appropriate tags, such as "Thursday Thoughts" or "Happy Friday." They can also tag the location of the photo, which lets viewers know where it was taken and adds depth to the story.

Snapchat

Snapchat is another social media application. It allows you to set a timer on photos and videos before they disappear. There are several ways to use Snapchat in the classroom with students. Many English language learners will love (or already love) Snapchat because it provides them an opportunity to express their feelings, emotions, and what they're currently doing without using complex sentences. Instead, they can record themselves speaking to an audience while adding fun and creative filters, texts, and emojis on the video or the photo.

"Stories" is a great Snapchat feature where people can create stories and share them with their followers or the world, depending on the user's privacy settings. Stories last twenty-four hours only, and they can be played as many times as possible within that timeframe.

Task:

1. Create a classroom Snapchat account for yourself. You can then add your students, as that's the only way you'll be able to see their photos and stories.
2. Have students create stories about what they're doing over the weekend.
3. Throughout the weekend, follow your students' stories, and be sure to post replies to them. For example, if they created a story about them on the beach with their family, then you can comment, "Wish I was there. Have a great time!"

4. Replying to student stories allows you to connect with their work and support their posts. This encourages students to write and share their voice with you.

COMMON CORE STATE STANDARDS AND DIGITAL WRITING

Digital writing with English language learners has many benefits, and one of the most practical benefits for teachers is that it also supports meeting Common Core State Standards (CCSS). According to Larry Ferlazzo's article "Collaborative Writing, Common Core, and ELLs," digital writing is supported by CCSS, as using technology to develop and publish writing helps with student collaboration. English language learners need to be in collaborative writing spaces in order for them to improve and practice their communication and writing skills.

CCSS focuses on three areas when it comes to literacy and writing: argumentative writing, informative or explanatory writing, and narration. Digital writing encompasses all these categories for students and provides an opportunity for them to practice and hone their skills using multimodal literacies.

Argumentative writing carries a lot of weight in the standards (Ferlazzo 2016). There is strong emphasis on the ability to read and understand an author's argument or explanation and main ideas and then develop a claim using text-based evidence to support the argument. Students are able to use various digital platforms to produce writing that meets the argumentative writing standards.

Informative and explanatory texts, according to Ferlazzo, are the kinds of texts that "help(s) readers *understand* how things work, why things happen, and what, in fact, did occur" (Ferlazzo 2016). Of course, some of the easiest forms of informative or explanatory texts can be reports, articles, short essays, instructions, summaries, and reviews. These are just a few examples of what students can produce or work with digitally.

Narrative writing is also a requirement of CCSS: "Use narrative techniques, such as dialogue, pacing, description, reflection, and multiple plot lines, to develop experiences, events, and/or characters" (*Common Core State Standards Initiative* 2016). As discussed earlier, digital writing allows students to imagine and create narratives and stories that meet these standards. Students are able to use various digital platforms to write their stories and use multimedia (recordings, music, sound) to enhance their dialogue.

There are also two areas in CCSS that support digital writing and the use of technology in the classroom. Under "Production and Distribution of Writing," the standards state: "Use technology, including the Internet, to produce and publish writing and to interact and collaborate with others" (*Common Core State Standards Initiative* 2016). This standard supports digital writing for English language learners, as collaboration is also one of the key practices that helps English language learners to learn better. Ferlazzo (2016) states that "collaborative writing has been found to be particularly helpful (PDF) to English-language learners (ELLs) in lowering anxiety and increasing self-confidence and motivation."

The other standard that supports digital writing and its process is under "Range of Writing." The standard states, "Write routinely over extended time frames (time for research, reflection, and revision) and shorter time frames (a single sitting or a day or two) for a range of tasks, purposes, and audiences" (*Common Core State Standards Initiative* 2016). This supports the idea of blogging and consistency in blogging. When students *consistently* write on an everyday basis, their writing strengthens and improves.

GLOBAL CONNECTIONS

What global teachers say about digital writing with their English language learners:

> "Publishing the voices of language learners helps people around the world connect to various cultures, learn about the struggles of im-

migrants, and hear incredible stories about assimilation. Blogs are the diaries of today, we will someday read as historic accounts of what young people felt and thought about various moments in history, including historic elections, refugee crisis, and through some of the big technology developments."—Shelly Sanchez Terrell, teacher-trainer and author of *The 30 Goals Challenge for Teachers* and *Learning to Go*

"Blogging is immensely valuable for ELLs. While we can expect it to produce significant writing gains, blogging also helps learners grow their listening, reading and speaking skills when incorporated with other activities. Blogging involves a great deal of reflective thought, enabling students to develop thinking skills in English. Furthermore, blogging gives them a voice, validating and celebrating their place in this world. The most rewarding aspect of blogging, however, is when students read their older posts and are able to see their growth."—Anabel Gonzalez, who has been teaching since 1996. She is a secondary ESL teacher for the Mooresville Graded School District in North Carolina. She teaches English language learners in grades 7 to 12 of various ethnic backgrounds, native languages, and English proficiency levels. Follow her on Twitter @amgonza.

"Digital writing is important to all students, but especially for ELL students because there are so many amazing ways to learn to read, write, and speak another language that doesn't involve worksheets. Power of technology lies in how we empower students to use their ideas and bring them to life in a variety of ways including digital stories, podcasts, and art pieces."—Meenoo Rami, author of *Thrive* and a national board-certified teacher who taught students English in Philadelphia for ten years at the Science Leadership Academy and in other public schools. Follow her on Twitter @MeenooRami.

"Twitter helps to establish an authentic audience for my students. My students actively tweet their classroom learning, thoughts and inspirations daily. In addition, they post quality work to the feed, which fosters a greater sense of pride and ownership in their work. My ELL students are motivated to construct meaningful, fluent texts so that their message may be easily related to the reader. Students are also excited to receive live, constructive feedback from other students and teachers, globally. Involvement in Twitter enables global connections, a community of sharing and a receptive, broad audience to my students."—Laurie Azzi, an elementary school teacher with the Ottawa Catholic School Board. She is a learning strategies teacher at Holy Family School, and her certifications are in special education and reading at the primary/junior levels. She incorporates many social justice themes into her teaching. Follow her on Twitter @laurie_azzi.

CHAPTER 4

Digital Citizenship and Digital Writing

DIGITAL CITIZENSHIP

Digital citizenship is a concept that helps teachers, education leaders, and parents to understand and navigate how to help students use technology appropriately. According to Mike Ribble (2016), digital citizenship is composed of nine elements: digital security (self-protection), digital communication, digital literacy, digital etiquette, digital law, digital rights and responsibility, digital health and wellness, digital access, and digital commerce. For the purposes of this book, the following elements are covered, as they relate to digital writing with English language learners: digital security, digital communication, digital literacy, and digital etiquette.

DIGITAL SECURITY

Many students, especially some older students (grades 9 to 12), may be hesitant about sharing their work with peers in the classroom, school, or online. Much of this hesitation may be due to the fact that they do not feel confident about their writing skills. However, some students will also be worried about their privacy and security, especially when sharing their work online.

Of course, permissions need to be granted by both the parents and guardians of the students and the students themselves before students share their work with the classroom, school, and online. (See textbox 4.1 for a sample letter of permission to parents.) It's crucial to let students know that they have a choice and options in setting permissions to public and private on any platform that they use to publish their work.

Familiarize students with how to change the settings of their accounts—on their blogs and social media—from public to private. For example, on YouTube, students have an option of making their videos unlisted, which means that only the people who have the URL can view it. In Instagram, accounts can be made private, which means that only the people whom students grant permission to follow can view their posts. A teacher can have students create a separate class account, adding only their classmates, with their permission, of course.

On most blogging platforms, you can choose to create a private or a public blog. Platforms that are specifically geared for education and contain a classroom management tool, such as Write About, EduBlogs, and the Writing Project, allow teachers and students to make their work public or private by going through a set of sharing permissions.

Bill Fitzgerald, director of privacy initiative at Common Sense Media, suggests that teachers consider the following when it comes to sharing students' work online:

> If you are going to share student images and work on social media, make intentional choices about what you share, how you share, and why you share. Additionally, ask your district about more granular policies for parents and learners. While the initial change might be hard, over time the more flexible rules will make your work easier, and increase trust between you, your students, and their guardians. (Fitzgerald 2016)

To ensure that all parents and students know their rights to privacy, leverage translation resources to help you communicate the process and the options that they have. This ensures that students and parents understand that they have a choice in making these decisions.

Remind students that, if they share their work publicly, then it will be the start of them creating their own professional digital footprint. Everything they publish should be representative of their true professional selves and reflect their learning in the classroom. It's also important to remember to keep students' accounts and blogs with credits only by their first names (if permission is obtained from parents and students to share online). Students' full names should not be included in the blogs. Their personal information should also be kept private.

DIGITAL COMMUNICATION

When it comes to digital communication, many students are hesitant to share their thoughts and ideas with their peers and online. Encourage hesitant and more reserved students to share their work with a couple of their peers before sharing online. This will ease them into the process of being vulnerable.

Digital communication is also different depending on the platform being used. For example, if your class is doing a Twitter chat to share their learning about a specific topic, then students will need to practice brevity and clarity in their tweets, as a result of the 140-character limit in a tweet. If the students are using Instagram to share a photo and write a post about it, then they have more room to write their descriptions and a picture to also convey deeper meaning.

As a result, consider how communicating digitally on different platforms can affect students' writing and communication skills. Are some students stronger communicators on Twitter than on Instagram? What do these students need to work on to improve on their weaker platform?

Struggling English language learners may benefit from being introduced to microwriting platforms, such as Twitter, Tumblr, and the Writing Project. Microblogging allows them to reflect and write short sentences about their thoughts and ideas. This can help students to feel less overwhelmed and makes the writing task much more manageable.

DIGITAL LITERACY

Digital literacy is the process of helping students to understand the importance of research and analyzing information online. For many English language learners, language can be a barrier when it comes to understanding the credibility of online resources. Help students to see the different elements that make up a credible source. Consider analyzing a website with them to look at the following details:

- *Author:* Who wrote the web page? What is his or her educational background? What is his or her experience in the field of this topic? Has he or she written anything in the past about this topic? Can we locate some of his or her other writing?
- *Publication:* What is the title of this publication? What topics does the publication cover? Do they have experts contributing to the publication? Is the publication academic? Are there scholars contributing to the publication? Does it contain research?
- *Date:* Sometimes the date can be a relevant factor when it comes to research. Consider if the source contains outdated information or recent research.
- *Point of View:* What is the overall goal of the publication? Who is presenting this information? Are there any commercials or advertisement on the website? What topics are they about? Does the source try to convince you of something? Which types of information does the source use to support the argument (e.g., data, research, opinions, anecdotal examples)?

DIGITAL RESEARCH ASSIGNMENT: "WHAT DOES YOUR SOURCE REALLY TELL YOU?"

Today's news is often witnessed first on such social media platforms as Facebook or Twitter. With trending hashtags, articles and images are often shared by the masses. Students need to understand how to best decipher a source and its credibility. This assignment will help students to look deeply at sources and see what they're really telling the reader between the lines. The objective of this assignment is to help students identify credible sources online and to analyze how they can best use those sources to support their arguments.

Task:

1. Ask students to form groups of three to four.
2. Next, ask groups to select a topic they're interested to learn more about. Topics can relate to current events or issues that are relevant to students, such as poverty, homelessness, immigration, and the refugee crisis.
3. Once they have selected their topics, they will need to research as a group and select a few websites that focus solely on their chosen topics. They can select three to four websites, and students can have a choice whether they analyze the websites together as a team or separately, with each member analyzing their own site.
4. Have students share their findings with their group members and the rest of the class, if there are any volunteers. In this way, students will benefit from seeing and hearing about the thought process that their peers went through when analyzing a source.

For the research assignment, feel free to use the previous categories as a guide for students to help them to analyze their sources. By helping students to analyze these pieces of information when it comes to their sources, you are helping them to become digitally literate and more prepared to be digital writers.

DIGITAL ETIQUETTE

Digital etiquette pertains to our online behavior and how we act in the digital world. Ask students to keep this in mind when sharing their writing online: Would you say this to a person in real life? If the answer is "no," then it shouldn't be published. Our digital footprints should represent who we are as people in real life. Therefore, it's important to remind students of what is considered appropriate and what isn't when it comes to digital writing and content.

Of course, a teacher can create a set of classroom rules and policies of what is appropriate to share online and what is inappropriate. However, often times it's better to discuss with students the real reason they should exemplify their real-life behavior online. Students will be able to see that these rules actually have meaning and aren't just arbitrary. For example, consider asking students whether they would say a hurtful comment about another student's writing to his or her face. Remind them that words have meaning in real life and online, and they can hurt others if they're not careful when choosing them. With that being said, culturally responsive teaching also calls for us to not practice "respectability politics" in the classroom.

WHAT IS RESPECTABILITY POLITICS?

Respectability politics happens when marginalized students are policed due to their behaviors, actions, and social values and, as a result, pushed to act and behave following mainstream values. This practice hurts students' confidence, self-esteem, and identities.

"Respectability politics is damaging and undermines the educational process by upholding white social values and norms of what is appropriate," writes Melinda D. Anderson, an education writer whose work focuses on the intersection of race and schooling. "Policing students of color in this way disregards and disrespects their language and self-expression, and affects their confidence and self-esteem—the result is a classroom that hinders learning and where students' success and performance is diminished." It is a slippery slope when teachers help students to identify what is considered appropriate and inappropriate to share online without changing the students' values and social norms.

Respectability politics often tone-polices marginalized students by telling them that their messages sound "angry" or "frustrated." Please remember that it's OK to elicit emotion in writing. In fact, we should encourage emotional writing, as it allows us to better understand our students. Sometimes, colloquial language is considered inappropriate when it comes to writing. It's crucial to remember, however, that colloquial language, especially to some English language learners, is part of their culture and upbringing. It's language that they use every day with their family and friends and is relatable to their everyday life and struggles. Taking that away from them also takes away from their identities.

FORMAL VERSUS INFORMAL WRITING

Digital writing is expanding its walls and parameters, and as a result, it's also changing our definition of what is considered formal writing. Sometimes a message may resonate with more readers if it sounds authentic and relatable. It's important to support students' authentic voice while still helping them to find the line between formal and informal writing.

When it comes to digital etiquette, the most vital aspect is to build a relationship with students. Understanding their backgrounds, culture, and social values will truly help in connecting with them and working together as a team to help them to succeed and become better digital writers.

SAMPLE PERMISSION LETTER TO PARENTS AND GUARDIANS

One of the most important aspects of digital writing is to protect the rights and privacy of students and their identities. Students' digital writing can be shared with an authentic audience as long as we have the permission of parents and guardians and students to do so. Often times, it's hard to obtain permission from parents if they are not

Textbox 4.1. Permission Letter to Parents and Guardians to Share Student Work, Videos, and Pictures
This letter was adapted from Jessica Liftshitz, 2016.

Dear Parents/Guardians,

Sharing our work with each other in the classroom has so many benefits for students. We also believe that sharing our work outside of the classroom walls, and in the digital world, can have such a great impact on students and the world around them. By sharing their work online to a wider audience, students will have an authentic audience and will feel that their work is relevant in the real world.

At the same time, I believe in respecting the rights and privacy of all students in the classroom. As a result, we will not be sharing any students' work, videos, or pictures without your permission. Please know that, when we're sharing online, we will never share students' full names in their work. And we will not post first names under any student videos, pictures, or images. Everything we'll share is positive and will be done in the hopes of creating positive change around us.

Please look carefully at the types of things that we might want to share with others. For each item, please select one of the four choices so that I know how comfortable you are sharing with others in our classroom (on the walls of our classroom or with groups of students or the whole class as examples to inspire others), in our school (on the walls of the hallways or other shared spaces within the building), and outside our school (on our class Twitter account, class website, or blogs read by other teachers).

Student Work (This may include writing samples, blog posts, written answers to questions, charts created, etc.)

_____ May not be shared
_____ May be shared within our classroom
_____ May be shared within our classroom and within our school
_____ May be shared within our classroom, within our school, and online with the world

Photographs/Images (This may include images taken in our classroom of a single student or of a group of students.)

_____ May not be shared
_____ May be shared within our classroom

_____ May be shared within our classroom and within our school
_____ May be shared within our classroom, within our school, and online with the world

Video (This may include video of students working, presenting, or speaking directly to the camera.)

_____ May not be shared
_____ May be shared within our classroom
_____ May be shared within our classroom and within our school
_____ May be shared within our classroom, within our school, and online with the world

I will keep records of how much each student and each family is comfortable sharing, and I will always work to make sure that nothing is shared that you do not feel comfortable sharing. If you ever feel that I have made a mistake and shared something that you wish I had not, please let me know, and I will make sure to correct it right away.

I am so excited to see all that we will share with each other, with our school, and with the world this year.

_____   _____
Signature   Date

---

familiar with different aspects of privacy settings and media sharing. Consequently, it's crucial that they are made aware of two facts:

- Parents have the right to know how their child's work is being shared.
- Parents have the right to know who is reading their child's work.

Writing a letter of permission to the parents and guardians of students might be the best way to communicate to them that your classroom is looking to expand their work to an authentic audience.

Textbox 4.1 shows a sample letter that was adopted from Jessica Liftshitz, a fifth-grade Chicago teacher. She wrote this letter to the parents and guardians of her students in order to get their permission to share students' work, pictures, and videos with the classroom and online.

What's very special about this permission letter is that it contains *four levels* of permission. The first level is whether the parents and guardians *do not* want to share their child's work online or in the classroom. The second level is whether parents and guardians wish to share students' work in the classroom only. The third level opens their sharing option to the classroom *and* school. And the fourth level of sharing opens students' work to the school and the digital world.

What's very interesting about having levels of permission is that these practices create a more inclusive and participatory classroom environment. Not everyone has to participate in digital writing, but there are options for students to share their work and, more importantly, with different types of audiences. In this way, parents and guardians do not feel pressured to opt their child into sharing their work with an audience that they're not comfortable with in order to avoid their child missing out on the assignment among their peers. They can still opt into sharing but with a more limited audience, and both options—the classroom and the school—are still considered an authentic audience.

CHAPTER 5
Creating a Culture of Connectivity

CREATING AN ENVIRONMENT FOR STUDENT VOICE

For many English language learners, the idea that their voice is an important part of the classroom culture and environment is not easy to grasp. In many cultures, students are used to being taught in a teacher-centered classroom, where the teacher's voice is the most important one in the classroom. It will take some time and effort on both the students' and the teachers' sides to really create an environment that cultivates student voice.

WHAT DOES AN ENVIRONMENT THAT SUPPORTS STUDENT VOICE LOOK LIKE? CONDITIONS THAT SUPPORT STUDENT VOICE

Choice

Providing students with a choice when it comes to reading and writing always helps to motivate and encourage student engagement with literacy. Many English language learners will not feel confident initially making their own choices when it comes to choosing a text to read or a topic to write about. Therefore, it's important that the teacher encourages students to do so at their own pace, with the teacher's guidance. Teachers can help students to see all the options they have and, from there, help them to make a decision by asking them questions about their interests, preferences, and passions. It's important to make this process of empowering student voice an ongoing one. This process also helps to build a stronger teacher–student relationship throughout the year.

Assessing Students' Needs and Wants

English language learners often come with one basic need: the need to know the language. However, it's vital that we don't overlook their learning styles, abilities, cultures, and preferences while we're helping them to grasp and understand the power of their own voice. When students' needs and wants are met, they're more inclined to want to engage and participate in their own learning. Moreover, by allowing students opportunities to learn while meeting their needs and wants, you'll be fostering a culture that supports student voice in the classroom.

Brainstorming

This is one of the easiest options to practice with students in order to empower them to believe that their voice is important and vital to the growth of their learning and their peers' learning. Brainstorming with students allows them to see that their ideas are valid, and more importantly, there is room for their ideas in the classroom—no matter how basic they might sound to them. Brainstorming also allows students to see that they can have an idea without putting too much effort into it. This is important because it instills in students that they have existing ideas, beliefs, facts, and opinions.

Inquiry

One can cultivate a nurturing environment for student voice by implementing inquiry-based learning in the teacher's pedagogy and lesson plans. Inquiry-based learning is often used in STEAM classes, but it's also a useful approach to try out with English language learners.

An important aspect of inquiry-based learning is authentic inquiry. This means that teachers do not have to wait for the right question to be asked. Any question the student asks can be used as a lead for further investigation. Encourage inquiry in the classroom by having students brainstorm questions they're curious about before the lesson. In fact, it's also a fun and engaging approach to have students brainstorm their questions and curiosities, and let them be the guide throughout the lesson. Help English language learners to feel confident to ask questions by providing them with prompts: "What do you think of . . . ?" "Who is . . . .?" "How does this work . . . ?" "Why is this important . . . ?"

Collaboration

Collaboration projects with English language learners, if not planned strategically, can leave students feeling isolated and unheard in the classroom. Teachers can encourage collaborative learning with their English language learners by observing the norms for group-work dynamics among students. By doing that, teachers will be able to meet students' differing learning needs and personalities among their peers.

Collaborations can start with small groups or peer "buddy" work. Group students strategically based on language proficiency. It's a good idea to pair more advanced language learners with beginner language learners so that they can benefit from communicating with each other. Collaboration allows students to feel more engaged in learning and helps students to form new relationships with their peers. These factors can help with improving self-confidence among English language learners, and as a result, they'll be more inclined to share their thoughts, ideas, and writing with the teacher and their peers.

Empathy

Helping students to develop empathy for each other in the classroom allows students to feel recognized, heard, and appreciated. There are many ways to help students to empathize with their peers.

Learning about each other's cultures, traditions, and countries can make a difference. Provide opportunities for students to discuss issues and tell stories about their backgrounds and where they're from. This allows students to get to know each other; form relationships; and, most importantly, feel safe to share their voice, thoughts, and ideas in the classroom.

Michael Fielding (2001) gives a good outline on the conditions that are needed in the classroom in order to foster and cultivate an environment for student voice (see table 5.1). This table is also useful when thinking about the role of student voice in school when it comes to policies, involvement, and engagement.

CULTURAL RESPONSIVE TEACHING AND DIGITAL WRITING

Our behavior is what we do; culture is how we do them. For example, we all eat lunch. *How* we eat lunch is what distinguishes one culture from another. Some cultures eat with forks; some eat with chopsticks; others eat with their hands. Many English language teachers know the importance of creating a culturally responsive classroom for their English language learners.

Cultural responsive pedagogy happens with intentionality and purpose. It's important that educators work to understand and confront their own personal biases and misconceptions. In this way, teachers are able to help students learn to their best ability. Jose Vilson, executive director of EduColor and a New York educator, suggests that cultural competence is an important component to the classroom and education because it allows us to form relationships with our students:

> Cultural competence is necessary because we can't teach students if we don't know the students we're teaching. Without cultural competence, we don't actually get to know the students. Time and again, we see how relationships allow for students to trust teachers as disseminators

Table 5.1. Evaluating the Conditions for Student Voice

Speaking	• *Who* is allowed to speak? • *To whom* are they allowed to speak? • *What* are they allowed to speak about? • What *language* is encouraged/allowed?
Listening	• *Who* is listening? • *Why* are they listening? • *How* are they listening?
Skills	• Are the skills of dialogue *encouraged and supported* through training or other appropriate means? • Are those skills understood, developed, and practiced within the *context of democratic values and dispositions*? • Are those skills *transformed* by those values and dispositions?
Attitudes & Dispositions	• How do those involved *regard each other*? • To what degree are the *principle of equal value* and the *dispositions* of *care* felt reciprocally and demonstrated through the reality of daily encounter?
Systems	• *How often* does dialogue and encounter in which student voice is centrally important occur? • Who *decides*? • How do the systems enshrining the value and necessity of student voice mesh with or *relate to other organizational arrangements* (particularly those involving adults)?
Organizational Culture	• Do the *cultural norms and values* of the school proclaim the centrality of student voice within the context of education as a shared responsibility and shared achievement? • Do the *practices, traditions and routine daily encounters* demonstrate values supportive of student voice?
Spaces & the Making of Meaning	• *Where* are the public spaces (physical and metaphorical) in which these encounters might take place? • Who *controls* them? • What *values* shape their being and their use?
Action	• What *action* is taken? • Who feels *responsible*? • *What happens* if aspirations and good intentions are not realized?
The Future	• Do we need *new structures*? • Do we need *new ways of relating to each other*?

"Students as Radical Agents of Change," Michael Fielding. 2001.

of knowledge. This is critical for ELLs, who often need school environments that allow teachers to make mistakes while they take on the process of acclimating to a new language. Embedded in cultural competence is the assumption that the cultures our students have is useful to the students' learning. That's a shift from the deficit models currently espoused in many classrooms. (Vilson 2016)

When it comes to writing, especially digital writing, there are many factors that need to be considered relating to students' cultural practices, beliefs, and traditions that teachers need to be mindful of in order to build strong student–teacher relationships based on trust, understanding, and kindness. So where do we start in building those long-lasting relationships that Mr. Vilson talks about?

In education, it's necessary for educators to focus on the pillars that create the necessary conditions for a culturally responsive classroom. In the Canadian Government's K12 Capacity Building series, these pillars are identified as three areas: institutional, personal, and instructional (Capacity Building Series 2013). Culture competence at the institutional level refers to administration and the leadership of the school. This also involves the values the school holds and processes. At the institutional level, it's vital to recognize how processes and cycles lead to marginalization of certain students.

Next, at the personal level, is the educators' own knowledge and awareness about who their students are, their backgrounds, their family life, and their cultures. What's necessary in this work is that culturally responsive educators are "self-aware" and acknowledge their own knowledge and biases when it comes to their students (Capacity Building Series 2013). This is necessary in helping to cultivate a culture understanding between the teacher and the student, as well as fostering an environment that is safe and empathetic.

The instructional dimension for culturally responsive teaching focuses on equitable pedagogical practices in the classroom and how they meet the learning needs of the students. This, of course, is in combination with personal and institutional.

HOW DOES THIS ALL RELATE TO DIGITAL WRITING AND MY STUDENTS?

Our understanding, knowledge, and perceptions of our students play a significant role in their success. If we truly work to form relationships with our English language learners, then we will come to understand the best possible practices to leverage and use in the classroom to support their success.

Writing opens many opportunities for students to share a lot of information about their interests, hobbies, talents, dreams, families, culture, beliefs, and much more. As a result, our recognition that students' culture is useful when it comes to their own learning is a step toward a culturally competent teaching practice. We must be able to see that what students bring with them to the classroom is an essential foundation in their future learning.

BEING MINDFUL OF CULTURAL DIFFERENCES

There are cultural differences that all teachers need to be mindful of when it comes to creating a safe environment for English language learners to write and communicate. With that being said, we also need to recognize cultural differences versus pure assumptions, biases, and prejudices. To find the balance between both is a challenging task and takes effort on the teacher's part, but it's worth it and a necessary part of the work when it comes to forming strong teacher–student relationships. Some common cultural differences may include the following.

Avoiding Eye Contact

In some cultures, it is a sign of disrespect to make eye contact with a person in a position of authority, such as a teacher. Many students might avoid eye contact when the teacher is addressing them.

This can be a bit of a change for teachers, as in Western culture, making eye contact is a sign of engagement or even understanding.

Solution: Check for understanding in different ways. One way to see if students understand the assignment and instructions is to do a strategy called "Concept Checking." Concept Checking is when you put the instructions in question form. For example: "When you comment on your peer's post, is it okay to write a negative comment publicly?"

Asking Questions

Many English language learners believe that asking questions is a sign of weakness. Some also don't ask questions because they may be afraid to ask out loud. Others may be hesitant to ask questions because they lack the language skills to convey their thoughts. This may especially be a bit difficult when it comes to understanding tech instructions for digital writing.

Solution: The best part about using technology in the classroom is that teachers can model the use with students. Guide the students through the process of creating a blog by showing them how you create your own. Take them to the computer lab and show them on the screen step by step how to create a blog, publish a post, edit, and so on. This will answer many questions, but most importantly, it'll show students that even the teacher may be unsure of how to do certain things, and that's normal.

Refusing to Engage in Discussion

Much of students' digital writing will most likely be opinion writing, argumentative, or analytical, based on a certain issue or topic. Some English language learners may hesitate to enter a discussion about current issues, events, and topics for several reasons. In some cultures, engaging in argumentative discussions may sound like it's challenging the teacher's authority.

Solution: Make sure to remind students of the reason you're having these discussions. Whether in writing or speaking, having discussions and being able to formulate an argument is an important part of developing critical thinking processes. Even more important, when students are able to engage in discussions or formulate their own argument, it means that they have an opinion about certain topics, issues, and events. And having opinions is what makes us the individuals we are, as opinions shape our beliefs and identities.

Refusing to Discuss Family Matters or Personal Issues

This is an issue that teachers can face with many students. However, with English language learners, we must be mindful that many, not all, come from immigrant and refugee backgrounds. Often times, there is trauma involved with this experience for the family and the student.

Solution: It's important to ask students whether they're able to discuss certain topics, especially if they hit close to home. It's also essential to provide parents with an opportunity to know their child's progress and which topics they will be writing about in the classroom. This can be communicated through a class newsletter, a note in the child's backpack, parent–teacher interviews, an e-mail, or even a phone call.

Culture competence in the classroom is a process. Teachers need to work together with administrators and leaders in their school to have open conversations about diversity, equity, and inclusion in their classrooms. Self-reflection is also a powerful tool to look inwardly at our own actions, beliefs, and perceptions to find solutions and improve ourselves for our students.

The following are some self-reflection questions to think about when your students start digital writing:

1. Am I creating a classroom atmosphere in which students feel respected by and connected to one another?

2. Does our learning environment support the personal experiences of each student?
3. Do my students feel supported in making choices when it comes to writing, engagement, and peer work?
4. Does the classroom atmosphere support all opinions, thoughts, and choices?
5. How can we, as a class, be more inclusive of all students' learning experiences?

CONNECTING WITH AN AUTHENTIC AUDIENCE

For many traditional classrooms, students' writing gets the teacher as an audience. And in some classrooms, the peers are the second audience. However, digital writing provides an opportunity for students' writing to move beyond the walls of the classroom. Connecting students to a wider audience than the teacher and their peers has many benefits. One of the biggest benefits of a wider audience is for students to recognize that their writing is relevant to their everyday life. When students see that their writing it relevant, they are more motivated and engaged in the writing process.

An authentic audience will also motivate English language learners to revise their work before publishing it. Students will care more about the quality of their writing if they know that more than their teacher will be looking at it and reading it.

For English language learners, the idea that their writing may reach others besides their teacher and peers may seem a little overwhelming at first. When one is learning a language, putting one's thought and ideas out for the world to see may make one feel vulnerable, so it's important for teachers to ease some of the stressors of digital writing by helping students to understand several core ideas:

- *They don't have to write for a wider audience right away.* For many students, it might be easier to start sharing their writing

with their peers at first. They can even share their work with other classrooms, if teachers are willing to collaborate. This helps to encourage students to see peer feedback, as it will be something they look forward to when opening their blogs. Commenting on others' posts can encourage students to write more and share their work more.
- *It's okay to make mistakes.* This, of course, can be applied to all learners, but English language learners especially need to be reminded of this fact because many of them will hesitate to make mistakes when writing. Let students know that it's OK for them to make errors while writing. The beauty of digital writing is that the students are able to go back to their earlier work and see the progress in their writing and language development. Digital writing also allows the writer to easily go back and edit their work if they notice an error or would like to change something in the content.

There are several ways to connect your classroom to an authentic audience:

- *Use Skype Classroom.* Skype Classroom allows you to connect with other classrooms globally. You can connect face to face and then continue this connection by sharing your work together. In this way, students are able to make global connections with other students who will read and comment on their work.
- *Create your own professional learning network.* In order for your classroom to connect globally, you as the teacher have to be connected. To be connected, create a blog or a Twitter account, and start sharing your writing with other educators. Join Twitter chats to meet educators who teach the same subject or grade level as you, and learn from them the different ways that they connect their classrooms.
- *Facilitate Google Hangouts with other classrooms.* The best part about creating your professional learning network is that

you can also meet those educators face to face. Facilitate a Google Hangout with a teacher and her classroom. If you find this intimidating at first, then you can first meet with the teacher and then connect your classrooms together.

English language learners will benefit from these global connections because they will be able to see that there are other kids just like them who are going through similar circumstances. It also introduces them to the concept that learning can happen outside the classroom and from people who are not in the classroom.

WHAT SHOULD ENGLISH LANGUAGE LEARNERS WRITE ABOUT?

Postcards to a Friend

Many English language learners will be missing their friends and family back home. Using social media to connect with their relatives and loved ones can be a powerful tool to engage them in writing and provide them with an authentic audience.

Task:

1. Ask students to choose one of their favorite social media apps that they use to connect with family and friends back home. Many students will choose Instagram or Snapchat. Both of these apps will allow students to share their stories or postings with you as well. Make sure to create a teacher account, if you're not comfortable using your personal account with them.
2. Have students share a photo or a short video of them experiencing something new and different. This could be a food, a place, or an activity.
3. Ask students to compose their post similarly to the way they would write a postcard. You can use the following template to guide students:

"Dear friends,
We're [or I'm] having a great time at [Where?]. We're [or I'm] doing [What? Describe activity.]. It's sunny here, which is a perfect weather for [What? Provide reason.]. This place is [What? Describe something unique.].
Wish you were here,
[Student's Name]

Note that this activity can be modified according to the app students are using. Some apps will have a character limit or a time limit. Also, it's important to remember that, for digital writing to be relevant, we need to remind students to be themselves. If they don't feel that they would say something similar to the example we provide for them, then they should not use that as an example. Instead, they should write what they feel they would say to their audience. Helping English language learners to find their voices is a process that works with love, guidance, review, and feedback.

Newspaper and Magazine

Introducing English language learners to the newspaper and magazine genre is an important part of literacy and digital literacy. Students will become familiar with the structure, composition, and point of view or perspective analysis once they complete several activities that require them to analyze the text in depth.

Task:

1. Have students choose an online publication of a newspaper or magazine that interests them. Provide a few examples for students who are not yet familiar with publications. Divide the examples into genres; for example, sports, entertainment, technology. This will help students to determine which subject area they're interested in and would like to learn more about. Ask students to examine the following elements in the article:

title, first paragraph, image, length. (Upper-beginner level: Have them share their initial thoughts about these elements.)
2. Upper-intermediate level: Next, have students write their own articles about a similar or different topic from those they chose in the same format as their articles.
3. Another strategy when using newspapers or magazines is to ask students to respond to the articles they chose. They can respond using different genres, such as letter writing, e-mail, text message, report, or another article of their own.

Students can blog their thoughts on the newspaper or magazine article activity. Or they can add it to their digital portfolios. A digital portfolio is similar to a blog, but the difference is using a platform specifically for digital portfolios. A digital portfolio is a collection of student work accumulated over time. Digital portfolios, along with writing, can also contain other achievements, such as interviews, awards, speaking opportunities, videos, and many other self-evaluative content. Along with Blogger and Wordpress, you can use such platforms as Evernote, Google Sites, and Weebly to create student digital portfolios.

Poetry

Poetry is a great way to develop English language learners' literacy skills, along with their creativity. You can have students write their own poems or replicate an example that you provide. It's usually a good idea to introduce them to reading poetry before writing poetry. Poetry is a bit complex in form, so familiarizing them with the form and structure can ease them into the poetry-writing process.

Task:

1. Provide a sample poem that's fairly simple and easy for students to read and understand, such as "Fog" by Carl Sandburg.

2. Ask students to replicate the poem using a subject they're interested in writing about. Feel free to provide them with prompts to get them started, such as "One of my favorite things to do is . . ." or "I really like [Person's Name] because . . ."
3. Once they publish their poems, they can share them with their peers, and their peers can provide their comments and feedback on their blogs.

It's important to make poetry writing relevant to the student's personal interests; in this way, they become more motivated and engaged to write. This strategy will also build a stronger teacher–student relationship because, when reading their work, the teacher will get to know more about students' interests, backgrounds, who they are, and where they come from.

Final Thoughts

Educators have the power to influence students and help them to believe that their writing matters. Students need to know that their writing can make a difference in their own lives and the lives of others. English language learners need to be empowered to use language as a tool to express themselves, their identities, their cultures, their backgrounds, and who they are as individuals.

Digital writing helps students to see that they have not lost connection with the real world. It'll help them to see that they in fact are still connected, very much, to the real world. It is this realization that will extend students' engagement and motivation in writing and will provide the drive for them to actually communicate and write effective ideas.

Being exposed to diverse ideas, socially and culturally, is such an important aspect in English language learners' communication, language development, and growth. With twenty-first-century learners, this type of exposure can and needs to occur in the digital world. Digital writing opens so many opportunities for English language learners to connect, collaborate, share, and exchange ideas locally within the school community and globally.

Digital writing is just a beginning step for students to create and develop their digital identities. By helping them to see the relevance of digital writing, you're also providing pathways for them to understand how to navigate the digital world and take ownership of it.

Many English language learners come from really difficult situations, and learning a new language, culture, and way of life is especially not an easy adjustment. Showing students that their stories matter, their voices are important, and that they can make a difference can be such a power realization for them. Students need to know that they are supported, appreciated, accepted, and loved in the classroom, school, and community. By providing them with different writing opportunities to express themselves and their identities, you will be connecting with them on a deep level of empathy and understanding.

So I challenge you today to start writing digitally with your students. You will see that they will begin to love writing, and their writing and communication skills will start to show a tremendous amount of improvement. Remember, you can start small. Start with Twitter and microblogging. Then take it one step at a time. You and your students will enjoy writing about topics you all care about. Once students see that their writing is relevant to everyday life, they will begin to understand and see that, through writing, they can make a difference in this world.

Bibliography

Anderson, Melinda. "Rusul Alrubail. Interview on policing students of color." Online, September 15, 2016.

Angay-Crowder, Tuba, and Youngjoo Yi. 2013. "Putting Multiliteracies into Practice: Digital Storytelling for Multilingual Adolescents in a Summer Program." *TESL Canada Journal* 30 (2): 36–45. Accessed June/July 2016.

"Ascilite 2015." Ascilite. Accessed September 20, 2016. http://www.ascilite.org.au/.

Bilash, Olenka. 2011. "Communicative Activities: What Counts as Speaking?" *Best of Bilash: Improving Second Language Education*. Accessed September July 27, 2016. http://www.educ.ualberta.ca/staff/olenka.bilash/best of bilash/communicative activities.html.

Common Core State Standards Initiative. 2016. "English Language Arts Standards » Writing » Grade 9–10 » 3." Accessed September 10, 2016. http://www.corestandards.org/ELA-Literacy/W/9-10/3.

Ferlazzo, Larry. 2016. "Collaborative Writing, Common Core, and ELLs." *Edutopia*. March 24. Accessed September 10, 2016. http://www.edutopia.org/blog/collaborative-writing-common-core-ells-larry-ferlazzo-katie-hull-sypnieski.

Fielding, Michael. 2001. "Students as Radical Agents of Change." *Journal of Educational Change* 2(2): 123–41. doi:10.1023/a:1017949213447.

Fitzgerald, Bill. 2016. "Encryption, Privacy, and Security." *FunnyMonkey*. Accessed September 30, 2016. https://funnymonkey.com/2016/encryption-privacy-and-security.

Gonzalez, Anabel. 2016. *Teaching Tidbits*. Accessed September 20, 2016. http://blog.teachingtidbits.com.

Lenhart, Amanda, Sousan Arafeh, Aaron Smith, and Alexandra Macgill. 2008. "Writing, Technology and Teens." *Pew Research Center: Internet,*

Science, and Tech. April 24. Accessed June 10, 2016. http://www.pewinternet.org/2008/04/24/writing-technology-and-teens.

McLoughlin, Catherine, and Mark J. W. Lee. 2007. "Social Software and Participatory Learning: Pedagogical Choices with Technology Affordances in the Web 2.0 Era." *Proceedings ascilite Singapore*. Retrieved February 10, 2011, from: http://www.dlc-ubc.ca/dlc3/educ500/wp-content/uploads/sites/24/2011/07/mcloughlin.pdf.

Mulligan, Christopher, and Russell Garofalo. 2011. "A Collaborative Writing Approach: Methodology and Student Assessment." *The Language Teacher* 35(3): 5–10. Accessed May 2016. http://www.jalt-publications.org/files/pdf-article/art1_13.pdf.

Ontario Ministry of Education. 2016. "Inspire." Accessed August 22, 2016. http://www.edu.gov.on.ca/eng/literacynumeracy/inspire/research.

Pew Research Center: Internet, Science, and Tech. 2016. Accessed September 20, 2016. http://www.pewinternet.org.

Purcell, Kristen, Judy Buchanan, and Linda Friedrich. 2013. *The Impact of Digital Tools on Student Writing and How Writing Is Taught in Schools*. Washington, DC: Pew Research Center's Internet and American Life Project. Accessed September 20, 2016. http://www.pewinternet.org/2013/07/16/the-impact-of-digital-tools-on-student-writing-and-how-writing-is-taught-in-schools-2.

Purcell, Kristen, Lee Rainie, Alan Heaps, Judy Buchanan, Linda Friedrich, Amanda Jacklin, Clara Chen, and Kathryn Zickuhr. 2012. *How Teens Do Research in the Digital World*. Washington, DC: Pew Research Center's Internet and American Life Project. http://www.pewinternet.org/files/old-media/Files/Reports/2012/PIP_TeacherSurveyReportWithMethodology110112.pdf.

Ribble, Mike. 2016. *Digital Citizenship: Using Technology Appropriately*. Accessed June 29, 2016. http://www.digitalcitizenship.net/Home_Page.php.

Son, Lisa K., Timothy Kenna, and Stephanie Pfirman. 2007. "A Metacognitive Pedagogy: The River Summer Project." *College Quarterly* 10, no. 2 (Spring). Accessed September 20, 2016. http://collegequarterly.ca/2007-vol10-num02-spring/son_kenna_pfirman.html.

Vilson L. Jose. "Rusul Alrubail. Interview on Cultural Competency." Online, September 10, 2016. Capacity Building Series, January 2013.

http://www.edu.gov.on.ca/eng/literacynumeracy/inspire/research/CBS_CBELL.pdf.

Zickuhr, Kathryn. 2013. "Reading, Writing, and Research in the Digital Age." *Pew Research Center: Internet, Science, and Tech.* November 4. Accessed September 20, 2016. http://www.pewinternet.org/2013/11/04/reading-writing-and-research-in-the-digital-age.

About the Author

Rusul Alrubail is the executive director of the Writing Project, a publishing platform and a community of student and teacher voices to empower advocacy in education about culturally relevant topics. She is also an education writer and a student voice advocate. Alrubail has taught English composition and literature to high school and college students for ten years. She has written for *Edutopia, Education Week, The Guardian, PBS Newshour, EdWeek Teacher, Teaching Tolerance,* ASCD's *Educational Leadership, Edsurge, Annenberg Learner Foundation, Medium,* and others.

    She's a TEDx speaker and a social media influencer on education, race, and equity. Her work focuses on teacher professional development and training, pedagogical practices in and out of the classroom, English language learners, equity and social justice, and media literacy as a means for professional development. You can find her work on her *Heart of a Teacher* blog (www.rusulalrubail.com) and connect with her on Twitter: @RusulAlrubail.

www.ingramcontent.com/pod-product-compliance
Lightning Source LLC
Chambersburg PA
CBHW030241170426
43202CB00007B/88